Collins

Very First Irish

DICTIONARY

Collins

HarperCollins Publishers

Westerhill Road
Bishopbriggs
Glasgow
G64 2QT
Great Britain

First Edition 2010

Reprint 10 9 8 7 6 5 4 3 2 1 0

© HarperCollins Publishers 2010

ISBN 978-0-00-735520-4

Collins® is a registered trademark of
HarperCollins Publishers Limited

www.collinslanguage.com

A catalogue record of this book is available
from the British Library

Typeset by Davidson Publishing Solutions,
Glasgow

Printed and bound in China by
South China Printing Co., Ltd

Acknowledgements

We would like to thank those authors and
publishers who kindly gave permission for
copyright material to be used in the Collins
Word Web. We would also like to thank
the Times Newspapers Ltd for providing
valuable data.

SERIES EDITOR
Rob Scriven

MANAGING EDITOR
Gaëlle Amiot-Cadey

PROJECT MANAGEMENT
Genevieve Gerrard

IRISH LANGUAGE CONSULTANT
Máire Nic Mhaoláin

DESIGN
Q2AMedia
Rob Payne

ILLUSTRATION AND IMAGE RESEARCH
Q2AMedia

Contents

a

adult
duine fásta
(daoine fásta *pl*)

after
i ndiaidh
after dinner
i ndiaidh an dinnéir

afternoon
tráthnóna
(tráthnónta *pl*)
at three o'clock in the
afternoon
ar a trí a chlog
tráthnóna

again
arís
Try *again*!
Triail *arís* é!

airport
aerfort

alien
eachtrán

alphabet
aibítir

ambulance
otharcharr
(otharcharranna *pl*)

and
agus
my brother
and me
mise **agus**
mo dhearthár

animal
ainmhí
(ainmhithe *pl*)

apple
úll
(úlla *pl*)

arm
lámh
(lámha *pl*)

ask
fiafraigh de
Ask somebody.
Fiafraigh de
dhuine éigin.

2

b

balloon
balún

banana
banana

baby
leanbh
(leanaí *pl*)

bad
droch-
bad weather
drochaimsir

basket
ciseán

bath
folcadán

bag
mála

ball
peil

beach
trá
(tránna *pl*)

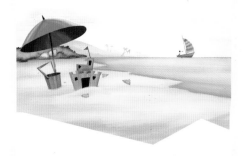

bed
leaba
(leapacha *pl*)

bedroom
seomra leapa

before
roimh
before three o'clock
roimh a trí a chlog

bicycle
rothar

3

big
mór
*a **big** house*
*teach **mór***

blanket
blaincéad

book
leabhar

blue
gorm
*a **blue** dress*
*gúna **gorm***

boot
buatais

bird
éan

birthday
breithlá

boat
bád

box
bosca

boy
gasúr

black
dubh
*a **black** car*
*carr **dubh***

body
corp

bread
arán

breakfast
bricfeasta

bridge
droichead

bring
tabhair

*Please **bring** me a glass of water.*
***Tabhair** gloine uisce dom le do thoil.*

brother
deartháir
(deartháireacha *pl*)

bucket
buicéad

burger
burgar

bus
bus
(busanna *pl*)

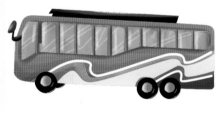

butter
im

butterfly
féileacán

buy
ceannach

*She's **buying** bread.*
*Tá sí **ag ceannach** aráin*

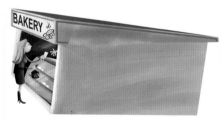

C

candle
coinneal
(coinnle *pl*)

castle
caisleán

cap
caipín

cake
cáca

car
carr
(carranna *pl*)

cat
cat

calendar
féilire

card
cárta

chair
cathaoir
(cathaoireacha *pl*)

carpet
cairpéad

cheese
cáis

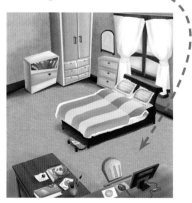

call
glaoigh ar
Call *this number.*
Glaoigh ar an uimhir seo.

chicken
sicín

carrot
cairéad

child
páiste

chocolate
seacláid

chopsticks
cipíní
itheacháin *pl*

cinema
pictiúrlann

circle
ciorcal

circus
sorcas

classroom
seomra ranga

clean
glan
*a **clean** shirt*
*léine **ghlan***

clock
clog

clothes
éadaí *pl*

cloud
scamall

clown
fear grinn
(fir ghrinn *pl*)

a
b
c
d
e
f
g
h
i
j
k
l
m
n
o
p
q
r
s
t
u
v
w
x
y
z

coat
cóta

computer
ríomhaire

cow
bó
(ba *pl*)

coffee
caife

cook
*He is **cooking**.*
*Tá sé **ag cócaireacht**.*

cry
goil
*Why are you **crying**?*
*Cad chuige a bhfuil tú **ag gol**?*

cold
fuar
*The water's **cold**.*
*Tá an t-uisce **fuar**.*

costume
feisteas

curtain
cuirtín

come
tar
***Come** with me.*
***Tar** liomsa.*

countryside
an tuath

a b c d e f g h i j k l m n o p q r s t u v w x y z

d

dad
daid
(daideanna *pl*)

dance
*I like **dancing**.*
Is maith liom
bheith ag
damhsa.

dangerous
contúirteach
*It's **dangerous**!*
*Tá sé **contúirteach**!*

daughter
iníon
(iníonacha *pl*)

day
lá
(laethanta *pl*)
*What **day** is it today?*
*Cén **lá** é inniu?*

dessert
milseog

dictionary
foclóir

difficult
deacair
*It's **difficult**.*
*Tá sé **deacair**.*

dinner
dinnéar

dinosaur
dineasár

dirty
salach
*My shoes are **dirty**.*
*Tá mo bhróga **salach**.*

do
déan
*What are you **doing**?*
*Cad tá tú **a dhéanamh**?*

doctor
dochtúir

door
doras
(*doirse pl*)

dream
brionglóid

dog
madra

downstairs
thíos staighre
I'm downstairs!
Tá mé thíos staighre!

dress
gúna

doll
bábóg

drink
ól
Drink *your milk.*
Ól *do chuid bainne.*

dragon
dragan

duck
lacha
(lachain *pl*)

dolphin
deilf
(deilfeanna *pl*)

draw
tarraing
Draw *a house.*
Tarraing *teach.*

DVD
DVD
(DVD-anna *pl*)

e

egg
ubh
(uibheacha *pl*)

evening
tráthnóna
(tráthnónta *pl*)
at six o'clock in the **evening**
ar a sé a chlog **tráthnóna**.

ear
cluas

elephant
eilifint

every
gach
every day
gach *lá*

Earth
an Domhan

email
ríomhphost

exercise
cleachtadh
(cleachtaí *pl*)

easy
furasta
It's **easy**!
Tá sé **furasta**!

eat
ith
I **eat** *a lot of sweets.*
Ithim *a lán milseán.*

empty
folamh
The bottle is **empty**.
Tá an buidéal **folamh**.

eye
súil
(súile *pl*)

11

f

father
athair
(aithreacha pl)

fire
tine
(tinte pl)

face
aghaidh
(aghaidheanna pl)

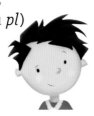

favourite
*Blue's **my favourite** colour.*
*Gorm an dath **is fearr liom**.*

fireworks
tinte ealaíne *pl*

fairy
sióg

find
faigh
*I can't **find** my bag.*
*Ní **fhaighim** mo mhála.*

first
céad
*the **first** day*
*an **chéad** lá*

family
teaghlach

fast
go gasta
*You walk **fast**.*
*Siúlann tú **go gasta**.*

finger
méar

fish
iasc
(éisc pl)

12

floor
urlár
*Sit on the **floor**.*
*Suigh ar an **urlár**.*

flower
bláth
(bláthanna *pl*)

fly
cuileog

food
bia

football
peil

forest
foraois

fork
forc

fridge
cuisneoir

friend
cara
(cairde *pl*)

frog
frog
(froganna *pl*)

from
ó
*a letter **from** my friend*
*litir **ó** mo chara*

fruit
toradh
(torthaí *pl*)

full
lán
*The bottle's **full**.*
*Tá an buidéal **lán**.*

funny
greannmhar
*It's very **funny**.*
*Tá sé an-**ghreannmhar**.*

g

ghost
taibhse

give
tabhair
Give me the book, please.
Tabhair dom an leabhar, le do thoil.

game
cluiche

giant
fathach

glass
gloine

garage
garáiste

giraffe
sioráf

glasses
spéaclaí *pl*

glove
miotóg

garden
gairdín

girl
cailín

glue
gliú

go
téigh
*Where are you **going**?*
*Cá bhfuil tú **ag dul**?*

goat
gabhar

grow
fás
***Haven't** you **grown**!*
*Nach tú a **d'fhás** ó shin!*

goodbye
slán

grapes
caora fíniúna *pl*

guinea pig
muc ghuine

grass
féar

goldfish
iasc órga
(éisc órga *pl*)

ground
talamh
(tailte *pl*)
*We sat on the **ground**.*
*Shuíomar ar an **talamh**.*

guitar
giotár

good
maith
*That's a **good** idea.*
*Sin smaoineamh **maith**.*

h

happy
sona
She is **happy**.
*Tá sí **sona**.*

head
ceann
(cinn *pl*)

hear
cluin
*I can't **hear** you.*
*Ní **chluinim** thú.*

hair
gruaig
*He's got black **hair**.*
*Tá **gruaig** dhubh air.*

hard
crua
This cheese is very **hard**.
*Tá an cháis seo an-**chrua**.*

hedgehog
gráinneog

hairdresser
gruagaire

helicopter
héileacaptar

hat
hata

hamster
hamstar

hello
dia duit

hand
lámh
(lámha *pl*)

have
*I **have** a bike.*
*Tá rothar **agam**.*

a
b
c
d
e
f
g
h
i
j
k
l
m
n
o
p
q
r
s
t
u
v
w
x
y
z

here
anseo
I live here.
Tá mé i mo chónaí anseo.

hide
She's hiding under the bed.
Tá sí i bhfolach faoin leaba.

holiday
saoire
We're on holiday.
Táimid ar saoire.

homework
obair bhaile

horse
capall

hospital
ospidéal

hot
te
a hot bath
folcadh te

hour
uair an chloig
(uaireanta an chloig *pl*)

house
teach
(tithe *pl*)

hungry
I'm hungry.
Tá ocras orm.

hurry up
déan deifir
Hurry up, children!
Déanaigí deifir, a pháistí!

husband
fear céile
(fir chéilí *pl*)

i

j

jigsaw
míreanna
(mearaí pl)

ice cream
uachtar reoite

jacket
seaicéad

job
jab
(jabanna pl)

idea
smaoineamh
(smaointe pl)

jam
subh

juice
sú

I'd like a glass of orange juice.
Ba mhaith liom gloine sú oráiste.

insect
feithid

jeans
brístí
géine pl

island
oileán

jump
léim
Jump!
Léim!

k

keep
coinnigh
*You can **keep** the book.*
*Féadann tú an leabhar **a choinneáil**.*

key
eochair
(eochracha *pl*)

kid
páiste

kind
cineálta
*a **kind** person*
*duine **cineálta***

king
rí
(ríthe *pl*)

kiss
póg
*Give me a **kiss**.*
*Tabhair dom **póg**.*

kitchen
cistin
(cistineacha *pl*)

kite
eitleog

kitten
piscín

knee
glúin
(glúine *pl*)

knife
scian
(sceana *pl*)

know
*I don't **know**.*
Níl a fhios agam.

a
b
c
d
e
f
g
h
i
j
k
l
m
n
o
p
q
r
s
t
u
v
w
x
y
z

19

l

laptop
ríomhaire glúine

leg
cos

lady
bean
(mná *pl*)

late
mall
I'll be **late** for school.
Beidh mé **mall** ag an scoil.

lemon
líomóid

lake
loch
(lochanna *pl*)

laugh
déan gáire
Why are you **laughing**?
Cad chuige a bhfuil tú **ag gáire**?

less
níos lú
I've got **less**!
Tá **níos lú** agamsa!

lamb
uan

letter
litir
(litreacha *pl*)

learn
foghlaim
I'm **learning** to dance.
Tá mé **ag foghlaim** damhsa.

lamp
lampa

light
solas
(soilse *pl*)

a b c d e f g h i j k **l** m n o p q r s t u v w x y z

like
I like cherries.
Is maith liom silíní.

lion
leon

listen
éist
Listen to me!
Éist liom!

little
beag
a little girl
girseach bheag

live
I live here.
Tá mé i mo chónaí anseo.

look
amharc
Look at the picture.
Amharc ar an bpictiúr.

lose
caill
I've lost my purse.
Chaill mé mo sparán.

lost
caillte
I'm lost.
Tá mé caillte.

loud
ard
It's too loud.
Tá sé ró-ard.

love
I love you.
Mo ghrá thú.

lucky
You're lucky!
Tá an t-ádh ort!

lunch
lón
(lónta pl)

a b c d e f g h i j k **l** m n o p q r s t u v w x y z

21

m

magician
draíodóir

make
déan
*I'm going **to make** a cake.*
*Tá mé chun cáca **a dhéanamh**.*

man
fear
(fir *pl*)

many
mórán
*He hasn't got **many** friends.*
*Níl **mórán** cairde aige.*

market
margadh
(margaí *pl*)

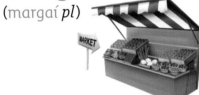

meal
béile

meat
feoil

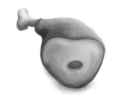

medicine
cógais *pl*

meet
buail le
*I **met** my friend in town.*
Bhuail mé le mo chara sa bhaile mór.

mermaid
maighdean mhara

mess
praiseach
*The place is a **mess**.*
*Tá an áit ina **praiseach**.*

milk
bainne

money
airgead

monkey
moncaí

monster
ollphéist
(ollphéisteanna *pl*)

month
mí
(míonna *pl*)
*What **month** is it?*
*Cén **mhí** é?*

moon
gealach

more
níos mó
*There are **more** girls than boys.*
*Tá **níos mó** cailíní ná buachaillí ann.*

morning
maidin
(maidineacha *pl*)
*at seven o'clock **in the morning***
*ar a seacht a chlog **ar** maidin*

mother
máthair
(máithreacha *pl*)

motorbike
gluaisrothar

mountain
sliabh
(sléibhte *pl*)

mouse
luchóg

mouth
béal

mum
mam
(mamanna *pl*)

music
ceol

n

name
ainm
(ainmneacha *pl*)

need
I need a rubber.
Tá scriosán uaim.

neighbour
comharsa
(comharsana *pl*)

newspaper
nuachtán

next
*the **next street** on the left*
*an **chéad sráid eile** ar clé*

nice
deas
*He's **nice**.*
*Tá sé **deas**.*

night
oíche
(oícheanta *pl*)

noise
callán

nose
srón

nothing
rud ar bith
*He does **nothing**.*
*Ní dhéanann sé **rud ar bith**.*

now
anois
*Do it **now**!*
*Déan **anois** é!*

number
uimhir
(uimhreacha *pl*)

123

nurse
banaltra

a b c d e f g h i j k l m **n** o p q r s t u v w x y z

o

of
de
*photos **of** my family*
*grianghraif **de** mo theaghlach*

old
sean
*an **old** dog*
***sean**mhadra*

only
aon
*my **only** dress*
***an t-aon** ghúna atá agam*

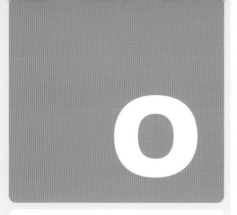

open
oscail
*Can **I open** the window?*
*An cuma má **osclaím** an fhuinneog?*

other
eile
*on the **other** side of the street*
*ar an taobh **eile** den tsráid*

p

page
leathanach

paint
péinteáil
*I'm going to **paint** it green.*
*Tá mé chun é **a phéinteáil** glas.*

paper
páipéar

parents
tuismitheoirí *pl*

passport
pas
(pasanna *pl*)

people
daoine *pl*

pasta
pasta

park
páirc
(páirceanna *pl*)

pet
peata

peas
piseanna *pl*

photo
grianghraf

pen
peann
(pinn *pl*)

party
cóisir

pencil
peann luaidhe
(pinn luaidhe *pl*)

piano
pianó
(pianónna *pl*)

a b c d e f g h i j k l m n o p q r s t u v w x y z

picnic
picnic

plane
eitleán

pocket
póca

plant
planda

picture
pictiúr

pocket money
airgead póca

plate
pláta

play
imir

I play tennis.
Imrím leadóg.

policeman
póilín

pirate
foghlaí mara

pizza
pizza

playground
páirc súgartha
(páirceanna súgartha *pl*)

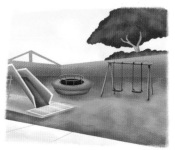

pony
capaillín

a
b
c
d
e
f
g
h
i
j
k
l
m
n
o
p
q
r
s
t
u
v
w
x
y
z

postcard
cárta poist

pretty
gleoite
a **pretty** dress
*gúna **gleoite***

puppet
puipéad

postman
fear poist
(fir phoist *pl*)

prince
prionsa

puppy
coileán

pushchair
bugaí linbh

potato
práta

princess
banphrionsa

pyjamas
pitseámaí *pl*

present
bronntanas

a b c d e f g h i j k l m n o **p** q r s t u v w x y z

q

r

rainbow
tuar ceatha
(tuartha ceatha *pl*)

queen
banríon
(banríonacha *pl*)

rabbit
coinín

read
léigh
*I **read** a lot.*
***Léim** cuid mhór.*

race
rás

quick
gasta
*a **quick** lunch*
*lón **gasta***

radio
raidió

ready
réidh
*Breakfast is **ready**.*
*Tá an bricfeasta **réidh**.*

quiet
suaimhneach
*a **quiet** little town*
*baile beag **suaimhneach***

rain
fearthainn

red
dearg
*a **red** T-shirt*
*T-léine **dhearg***

29

remember
I can't remember his name.
Ní cuimhin liom *a ainm.*

right
ceart
*It isn't the **right** size.*
*Níl sé an mhéid **cheart**.*

robot
robat

rocket
roicéad

restaurant
bialann

ring
fáinne

river
abhainn
(aibhneacha *pl*)

rocket
roicéad

room
seomra

rice
rís

rich
saibhir
*He's very **rich**.*
*Tá sé an-**saibhir**.*

road
bóthar
(bóithre *pl*)

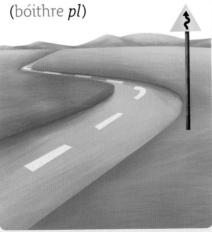

run
rith
Run!
Rith!

a b c d e f g h i j k l m n o p q r s t u v w x y z

S

sandwich
ceapaire

say
abair
*What **did you say**?*
*Cad a **dúirt tú**?*

sad
buartha
*Don't be **sad**.*
*Ná bí **buartha**.*

school
scoil
(scoileanna pl)

same
céanna
*They're in the **same** class.*
*Tá siad sa rang **céanna**.*

scissors
siosúr sg

sand
gaineamh

sea
farraige

second
dara

see
feic
*I **can see** her car.*
Feicim a carr.

sell
díol
*He's **selling** his bike.*
*Tá sé **ag díol** a rothair.*

a
b
c
d
e
f
g
h
i
j
k
l
m
n
o
p
q
r
s
t
u
v
w
x
y
z

send
cuir
Send *me an email.*
Cuir *ríomhphost chugam.*

shadow
scáth
(scáthanna *pl*)

sheep
caora
(caoirigh *pl*)

shirt
léine
(léinte *pl*)

shoe
bróg

shop
siopa

shorts
brístí gearra *pl*

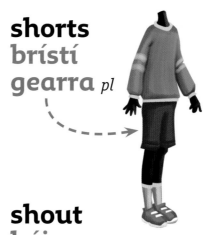

shout
béic
Don't shout, *children!*
Ná bígí ag béiceadh,
a pháistí!

show
taispeáin
Show *me the photos.*
Taispeáin *na grianghraif dom.*

shower
cithfholcadán

sick
tinn
*He is **sick.***
*Tá sé **tinn.***

sing
can
*I **sing** in the choir.*
***Canaim** sa chór.*

sister
deirfiúr
(deirfiúracha *pl*)

a b c d e f g h i j k l m n o p q r **s** t u v w x y z

32

sit
suigh
*Can I **sit** here?*
*An bhféadfainn **suí** anseo?*

skin
craiceann
(craicne *pl*)

skirt
sciorta

sky
spéir
(spéartha *pl*)

sleep
codail
*My cat **sleeps** in a box.*
***Codlaíonn** mo chat i mbosca.*

slow
mall
*The tortoise is very **slow**.*
*Tá an toirtís an-**mhall**.*

smell
*Mmm, that **smells** good!*
*Mmm, tá **boladh** deas as!*

smile
miongháire

snail
seilide

snake
nathair
(nathracha *pl*)

snow
sneachta

snowman
fear sneachta
(fir shneachta *pl*)

soap
gallúnach

a
b
c
d
e
f
g
h
i
j
k
l
m
n
o
p
q
r
s
t
u
v
w
x
y
z

sock
stoca

soup
anraith

spoon
spúnóg

sport
spórt

sofa
tolg

spaceship
spasárthach

square
cearnóg

son
mac
(mic *pl*)

speak
Do you speak French?
An bhfuil Fraincis **agat**?

stairs
staighre

spider
damhán alla

sorry
I'm sorry!
Tá brón orm!

star
réalta

a
b
c
d
e
f
g
h
i
j
k
l
m
n
o
p
q
r
s
t
u
v
w
x
y
z

station
stáisiún

stick
greamaigh

Stick it onto the paper.
Greamaigh den pháipéar é.

sticker
greamán

stone
cloch

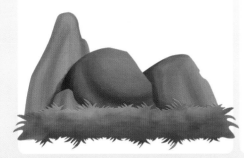

stop
stad

Stop, that's enough!
Stad de sin!

story
scéal
(scéalta *pl*)

street
sráid
(sráideanna *pl*)

strong
láidir

She's very **strong**.
Tá sí an-láidir.

sun
grian

supermarket
ollmhargadh
(ollmhargaí *pl*)

surprise

What a surprise!
Níor shamhlaigh mé riamh é!

swim

I can swim.
Tá snámh agam.

swimming pool
linn snámha
(linnte snámha *pl*)

35

tall
ard
*a very **tall** building*
*foirgneamh an-**ard***

telephone
guthán

table
tábla

television
teilifís

take
tóg
***Take** a card.*
***Tóg** cárta.*

taxi
tacsaí

text message
teachtaireacht téacs

tea
tae

thank you
go raibh maith agat

talk
*You **talk** too much.*
Tá an iomarca cainte agat.

teddy bear
béirín

36

think
smaoinigh
*What are you **thinking** about?*
*Cad air a bhfuil tú **ag smaoineamh**?*

third
tríú
*the **third** prize*
*an **tríú** duais*

tie
carbhat

tiger
tíogar

tired
I'm tired.
Tá tuirse orm.

toast
tósta

today
inniu
*It's Monday **today**.*
***Inniu** an Luan.*

together
le chéile

toilet
leithreas

tomato
tráta

tomorrow
amárach
*See you **tomorrow**!*
*Feicfidh mé **amárach** thú!*

tooth
fiacail
(fiacla pl)

toothbrush
scuab fiacla

a b c d e f g h i j k l m n o p q r s **t** u v w x y z

37

toothpaste
taos fiacla

toy
bréagán

tree
crann

tortoise
toirtís

tractor
tarracóir

triangle
triantán

towel
tuáille

train
traein
(traenacha *pl*)

trousers
treabhsar

town
baile mór
(bailte móra *pl*)

treasure
stór
(stórtha *pl*)

T-shirt
T-léine
(T-léinte *pl*)

a b c d e f g h i j k l m n o p q r s **t** u v w x y z

u

umbrella
scáth fearthainne
(scáthanna fearthainne *pl*)

understand
tuig
*I don't **understand**.*
*Ní **thuigim**.*

uniform
éide

up
*The cat is **up** on the roof.*
*Tá an cat **in airde** ar an díon.*

upstairs
suas staighre
*to go **upstairs***
*dul **suas staighre***

v

vanilla
fanaile
***vanilla** ice cream*
*uachtar reoite **fanaile***

vegetable
glasra

very
an-
***very** small*
***an**-bheag*

vet
tréidlia
(tréidlianna *pl*)

video game
físchluiche

visit
*We're going **to visit** the castle.*
*Táimid chun **cuairt** **a thabhairt** ar an gcaisleán.*

w

wait
fan
Wait for me!
Fan liomsa!

wake up
múscail
Wake up!
Múscail!

walk
siúil
He walks fast.
Siúlann sé go gasta.

wall
balla
There are posters on the wall.
Tá póstaeir ar an mballa.

want
Do you want some cake?
An bhfuil *píosa cáca uait?*

warm
te
warm *water*
uisce **te**

wash
nigh
Wash *your hands!*
Nigh *do lámha!*

watch
uaireadóir

water
uisce

wave
tonn
(tonnta *pl*)

wear
caith
He's **wearing** *a hat.*
Tá sé **ag caitheamh** *hata.*

webcam
ceamara gréasáin

website
suíomh gréasáin
(suíomha gréasáin *pl*)

week
seachtain
(seachtainí *pl*)
I play football every **week**.
Imrím peil gach seachtain.

weekend
deireadh seachtaine
(deirí seachtaine *pl*)
I play tennis at the **weekend**.
Imrím leadóg ag an deireadh seachtaine.

welcome
fáilte

well
go maith
*She played **well**.*
*D'imir sí **go maith**.*

wheelchair
cathaoir rothaí
(cathaoireacha rothaí *pl*)

white
bán
*I'm wearing a **white** shirt.*
*Léine **bhán** atá orm.*

wife
bean chéile
(mná céilí *pl*)

wild
fiáin
*a **wild** animal*
*ainmhí **fiáin***

win
buaigh
*I always **win**.*
***Buaim** i gcónaí.*

wind
gaoth

window
fuinneog

winner
buaiteoir

wolf
mac tíre
(mic thíre *pl*)

world
domhan

witch
cailleach

woman
bean
(mná *pl*)

write
scríobh
*I'm **writing** to my friend.*
*Tá mé **ag scríobh** chuig mo chara.*

with
le
*Come **with me**.*
*Tar **liomsa**.*

word
focal

wrong
mícheart
*That answer is **wrong**.*
*Tá an freagra sin **mícheart**.*

work
obair
She works in a bank.
*Tá sí **ag obair** i mbanc.*

without
gan
***without** a coat*
***gan** chóta*

a b c d e f g h i j k l m n o p q r s t u v **w** x y z

x

y

young
óg
She's young.
Tá sí óg.

X-ray
x-gha
(x-ghathanna *pl*)

year
bliain
(blianta *pl*)
I'm seven years old.
Tá mé seacht mbliana d'aois.

z

yellow
buí
I'm wearing yellow shorts.
Tá brístí gearra buí orm.

zebra
séabra

xylophone
xileafón

yesterday
inné
I was late yesterday.
Bhí mé mall inné.

zoo
zú
(zúnna *pl*)

Ainmhithe
Animals

cat
cat

crogall
crocodile

séabra
zebra

eilifint
elephant

nathair
snake

piongain
penguin

sioráf
giraffe

mac tíre
wolf

laghairt
lizard

capall
horse

44

bó
cow

madra
dog

leon
lion

dobhareach
hippo

panda
panda

tíogar
tiger

éan
bird

coinín
rabbit

iasc
fish

caora
sheep

moncaí
monkey

cangarú
kangaroo

45

Baile mór
Town

siopa báicéara
bakery

banc
bank

ollmhargadh
supermarket

sráid
street

siopa
shop

ospidéal
hospital

stáisiún
station

oifig an phoist
post office

páirc
park

eitleán
plane

bus
bus

traein
train

carr
car

rothar
bike

bialann
restaurant

pictiúrlann
cinema

músaem
museum

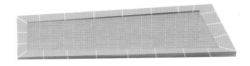
cosán
pavement

margadh
market

47

Scoil
School

scriosán
rubber

bioróir
pencil sharpener

cás peann luaidhe
pencil case

dalta
pupil

mála scoile
schoolbag

áit súgartha
playground

sleamhnán
slide

timpeallán spraoi
roundabout

luascán
swing

seomra ranga
classroom

48

peann luaidhe
pencil

peann
pen

rialóir
ruler

cóipleabhar
exercise book

póstaer
poster

cathaoir
chair

ríomhaire
computer

deasc
desk

cófra
cupboard

clár bán idirghníomhach
interactive whiteboard

múinteoir
teacher

49

Teach
House

áiléar
attic

garáiste
garage

seomra leapa
bedroom

seomra bia
dining room

seomra folctha
bathroom

staighre
stairs

seomra teaghlaigh
living room

díon
roof

cistin
kitchen

seomra staidéir
study

doras
door

fuinneog
window

gairdín
garden

50

Seomra leapa
Bedroom

clog aláraim
alarm clock

leaba
bed

bréagán
toy

ríomhaire
computer

seinnteoir dlúthdhioscaí
CD player

cóifrín cois leapa
bedside table

cófra tarraiceán
chest of drawers

seilf leabhar
bookshelf

cuirtíní
curtains

vardrús
wardrobe

lampa
lamp

scáthán
mirror

pitseámaí
pyjamas

piliúr
pillow

duivé
duvet

slipéir
slippers

deasc
desk

51

Bia
Food

brioscáin phrátaí
crisps

briosca
biscuit

uisce
water

pláta
plate

cupán
cup

scian
knife

forc
fork

spúnóg
spoon

úll
apple

oráiste
orange

cairéid
carrots

sailéad
salad

im
butter

cáis
cheese

sceallóga
chips

uachtar reoite
ice cream

arán
bread

burgar
burger

sicín
chicken

sú torthaí
fruit juice

bainne
milk

pasta
pasta

ceapaire
sandwich

pizza
pizza

ris
rice

seacláid
chocolate

53

Lá breithe sona!
Happy birthday!

cáca
cake

cara
friend

mamó
grandma

daideo
granddad

cárta
card

brioscáin phrátaí
crisps

líomanáid
lemonade

54

balún
balloon

ceamara
camera

coinneal
candle

daid
dad

mam
mum

deirfiúr
sister

deartháir 55
brother

bronntanas
present

milseáin
sweets

Corp
Body

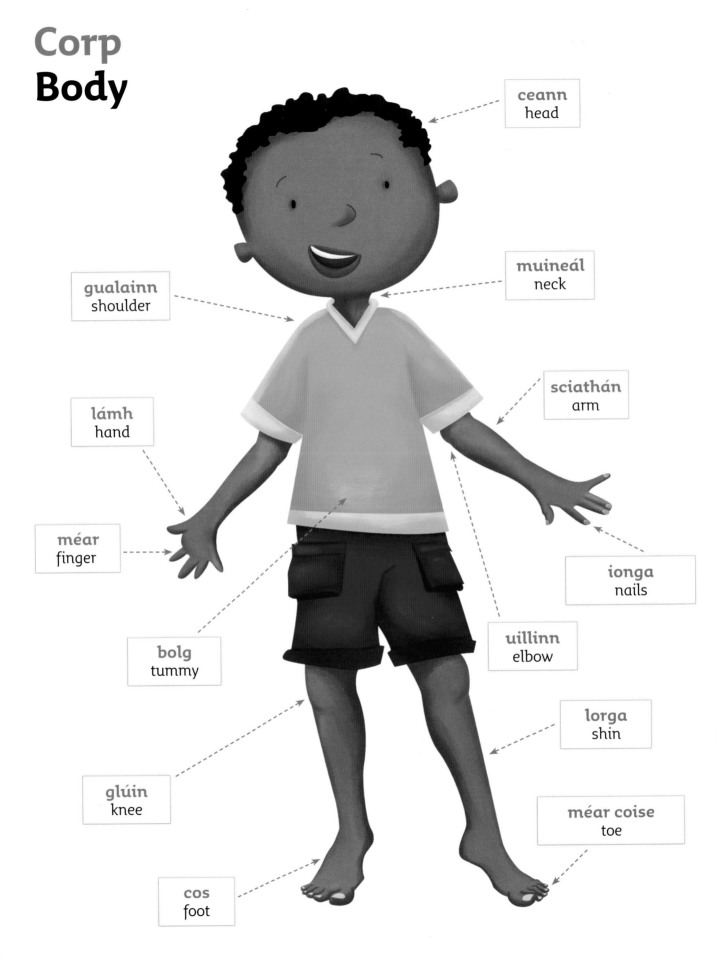

ceann
head

muineál
neck

gualainn
shoulder

sciathán
arm

lámh
hand

méar
finger

ionga
nails

bolg
tummy

uillinn
elbow

lorga
shin

glúin
knee

méar coise
toe

cos
foot

Aghaidh
Face

gruaig
hair

súil
eye

cluas
ear

liopa
lip

srón
nose

leiceann
cheek

béal
mouth

fiacla
teeth

smig
chin

Dathanna
Colours

dubh
black

gorm
blue

donn
brown

glas
green

liath
grey

dúghorm
navy

flannbhuí
orange

bándearg
pink

corcra
purple

dearg
red

bán
white

buí
yellow

Éadaí
Clothes

 léine aclaíochta sweatshirt

 gúna dress

 seaicéad jacket

 brístí géine jeans

 scairf scarf

 miotóga gloves

 cóta coat

 geansaí jumper

 bróga shoes

 léine shirt

 stocaí socks

 caipín cap

 caipín olla woolly hat

 barrchóir top

 riteoga tights

 treabhsar trousers

 T-léine T-shirt

 sciorta skirt

bróga spóirt trainers

59

Cur síos ar dhaoine
Describing people

Tá mé te.
I'm hot.

Tá mé fuar.
I'm cold.

Tá codladh orm.
I'm sleepy.

Tá ocras orm.
I'm hungry.

Tá tart orm.
I'm thirsty.

Tá sí sona.
She's happy.

Tá mé buartha.
I'm sad.

Tá mé meabhrach.
I'm intelligent.

Tá eagla orm.
I'm scared.

Tá mé tinn.
I'm sick.

Tá mé cainteach.
I'm chatty.

Tá fearg orm.
I'm angry.

Imrím spórt.
I'm sporty.

Tá sí cúthail.
She's shy.

Tá sé leadránach.
He's boring.

Tá mé bréan de seo.
I'm bored.

Tá mé deas
I'm nice.

Conversations
Comhráite

Slán!
Goodbye!

Cad chuige a bhfuil tú ag gol?
Why are you crying?

Tá mé caillte.
I'm lost.

Le do thoil!
Please!

Dia duit!
Hello!

Cén t-am a thosaíonn an scoil?
When does school start?

Cé mhéad deartháir agus deirfiúr agat?
How many brothers and sisters do you have?

Ar a naoi a chlog.
At nine o'clock.

Tá deartháir amháin agam agus beirt deirfiúracha.
I have one brother and two sisters.

Cad is maith leat a dhéanamh?
What do you enjoy doing?

Is maith liom...
I like...

bheith ag damhsa
dancing

canadh
singing

an giotár a sheinm
playing guitar

an pianó a sheinm
playing piano

dul ag rothaíocht
riding my bike

bheith ag
imirt peile
playing football

cispheil a imirt
playing basketball

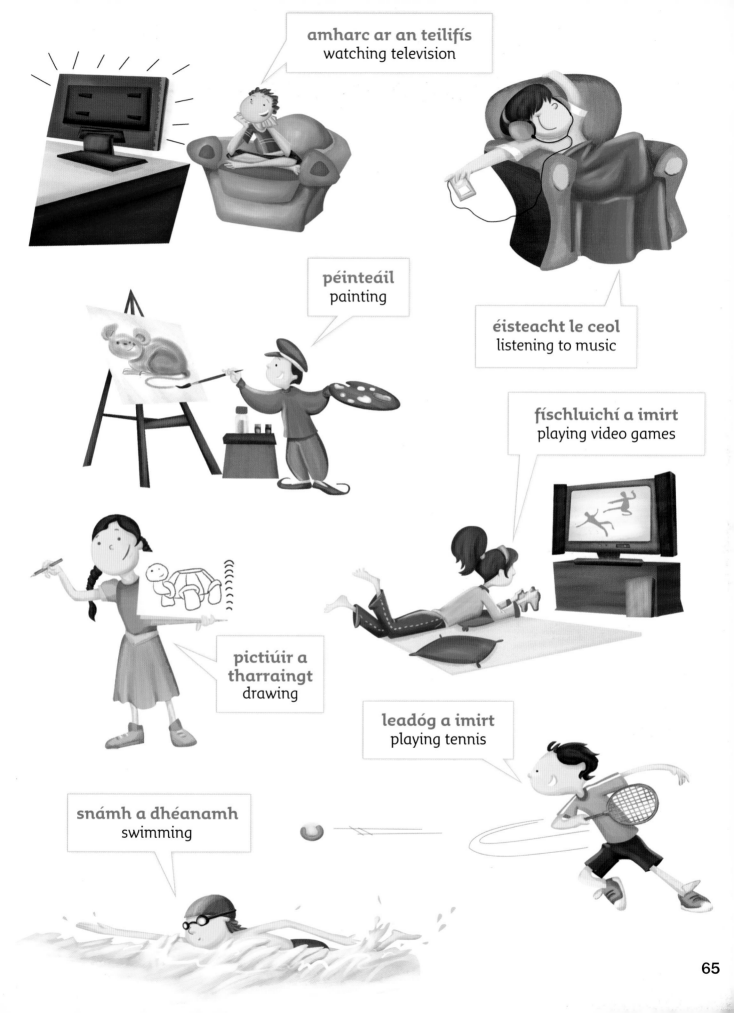

amharc ar an teilifís
watching television

éisteacht le ceol
listening to music

péinteáil
painting

físchluichí a imirt
playing video games

pictiúir a tharraingt
drawing

leadóg a imirt
playing tennis

snámh a dhéanamh
swimming

65

Na míonna
Months of the year

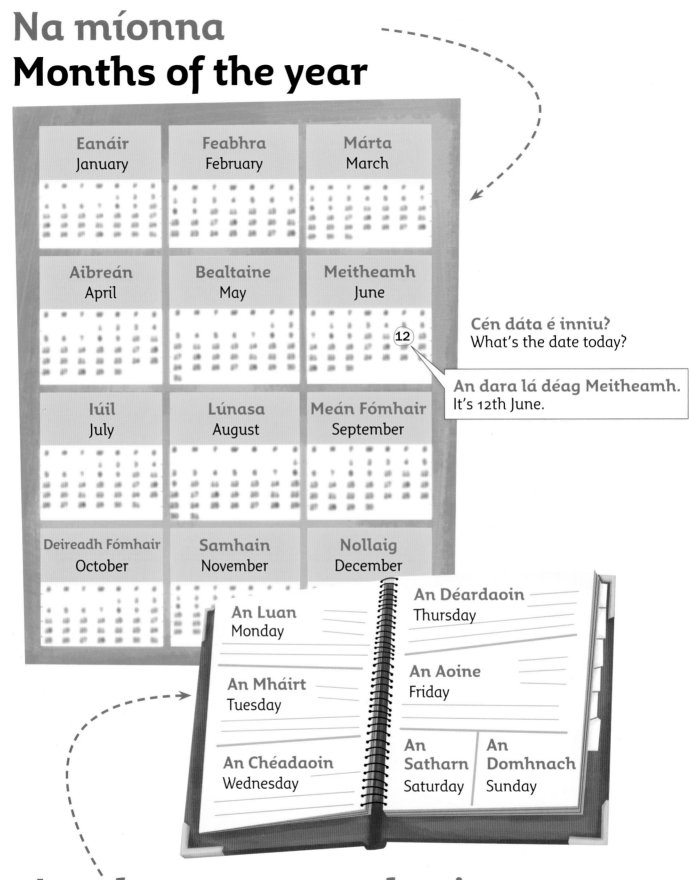

Eanáir January	Feabhra February	Márta March
Aibreán April	Bealtaine May	Meitheamh June
Iúil July	Lúnasa August	Meán Fómhair September
Deireadh Fómhair October	Samhain November	Nollaig December

Cén dáta é inniu?
What's the date today?

An dara lá déag Meitheamh.
It's 12th June.

An Luan
Monday

An Mháirt
Tuesday

An Chéadaoin
Wednesday

An Déardaoin
Thursday

An Aoine
Friday

An Satharn
Saturday

An Domhnach
Sunday

Laethanta na seachtaine
Days of the week

Na séasúir
Seasons

earrach
spring

samhradh
summer

fómhar
autumn

geimhreadh
winter

Cén aimsir atá ann?
What's the weather like?

Tá sé scamallach.
It's cloudy.

Tá sé fuar.
It's cold.

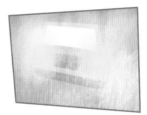
Tá ceo ann.
It's foggy.

Tá sé ag cur seaca.
It's icy.

Tá sé gruama.
It's overcast.

Tá sé ag cur fearthainne.
It's raining.

Tá sé ag cur sneachta.
It's snowing.

Tá stoirm ann.
It's stormy.

Tá sé gaofar.
It's windy.

Tá sé te.
It's hot.

Tá sé grianmhar.
It's sunny.

Tá sé go breá.
It's nice.

Uimhreacha
Numbers

0 a náid	10 a deich	20 fiche	81 ochtó a haon
1 a haon	11 a haon déag	21 fiche a haon	82 ochtó a dó
2 a dó	12 a dó dhéag	22 fiche a dó	90 nócha
3 a trí	13 a trí déag	30 tríocha	91 nócha a haon
4 a cea-thair	14 a cea-thairdéag	40 daichead	100 céad
5 a cúig	15 a cúig déag	50 caoga	101 céad a haon
6 a sé	16 a sé déag	60 seasca	200 dhá chéad
7 a seacht	17 a seacht déag	70 seachtó	250 dhá chéad is caoga
8 a hocht	18 a hocht déag	71 seachtó a haon	1000 míle
9 a naoi	19 a naoi déag	72 seachtó a dó	2000 dhá mhíle
		80 ochtó	1000000 milliún

Cén t-am atá sé?
What's the time?

a haon a chlog
one o'clock

deich i ndiaidh a haon
ten past one

ceathrú i ndiaidh a haon
a quarter past one

leath i ndiaidh a haon
half past one

fiche go dtí a dó
twenty to two

ceathrú go dtí a dó
a quarter to two

Cén t-am...?
What time...?

ag ceathrú i ndiaidh a haon déag
at quarter past eleven

ag meánlae
at midday

ag a haon tráthnóna
at one o'clock in the afternoon

ag a sé a chlog
at six o'clock

ag ceathrú go dtí a naoi san oíche
at quarter to nine

ag meán oíche
at midnight

Cá bhfuil siad?
Where are they?

Tá an madra **taobh thiar** den teilifíseán.
The dog is **behind** the television.

Tá an cat **in airde** ar an díon.
The cat is **up** on the roof.

Tá an carr **os comhair** an tí.
The car is **in front of** the house.

Tá an luchóg **thíos** sa siléar.
The mouse is **down** in the cellar.

Tá an t-éan **i bhfad ón** gcrann.
The bird is **far away from** the tree.

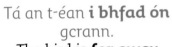

Tá an crann **in aice leis** an teach.
The tree is **near** the house.

Tá sí ag dul **ón** teach **go dtí** an scoil.
She is going **from** the house **to** the school.

Tá sé **anseo**.
He is **here**.

Tá sí **ansin**.
She is **there**.

Fan liom **taobh amuigh**.
Wait for me **outside**.

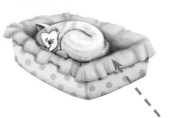

Tá an cat **sa** bhosca.
The cat is **in** the box.

Tá sé ag teacht **amach as** an ngairdín.
He is coming **out of** the garden.

Tá sé ag léim **isteach sa** linn.
He is jumping **into** the pool.

Tá sí **istigh sa** teach.
She's **inside** the house.

Tá an carr ag casadh **ar clé**.
The car is turning **left**.

Tá an rothar ag casadh **ar dheis**.
The bike is turning **right**.

Tá an cat **faoin** tábla.
The cat is **under** the table.

Tá an madra **idir** an dá chat.
The dog is **between** the two cats.

Tá an banc **ar aghaidh** na bialainne.
The bank is **opposite** the restaurant.

Tá an madra **ar** an tolg.
The dog is **on** the sofa.

Tá an siopa báicéara **taobh leis** an ollmhargadh.
The bakery is **next to** the supermarket.

71

Nouns

Words such as 'apple', 'room' and 'friend' refer to things or persons and are called **nouns**.

In Irish you do not need a special word (like 'a' in English) to show you mean one thing or person (**singular**). **Cara** means 'friend' or 'a friend'. 'The friend' is **an cara**.

When more than one person or thing is meant (**plural**), the ending of the noun changes. There are various rules for normal plurals in Irish. But some nouns form plurals in other ways. These are **irregular plurals** and are shown in this dictionary with a small *pl*. For example:

cow
bó
(ba *pl*)

flower
bláth
(bláthanna *pl*)

The word for 'the' changes in the plural too, so 'the cows' is **na ba**.

All nouns are either **masculine** or **feminine** in Irish. You can check in the index to see if a word is masculine (**m**) or feminine (**f**). This is important because it can affect the beginning of the noun itself after **an** 'the'.

- Masculine nouns do not generally change after **an**. 'The dress' is **an gúna**, and 'the dog' is **an madra**.

  However, 'a bird' is **éan**, but 'the bird' is **an t-éan**, because **éan** begins with a vowel.

- Feminine nouns mostly change their beginnings after **an**. 'A shoulder' is **gualainn**, but 'the shoulder' is **an ghualainn**. 'A fly' is **cuileog**, but 'the fly' is **an chuileog**. Feminine nouns beginning with a vowel do not change their first letter after **an**. 'Elbow' is **uillinn**, and 'the elbow' is **an uillinn**.

Adjectives

An **adjective** is a word such as 'big' **mór**, 'blue' **gorm**, or 'clean' **glan** which describes or tells more about a noun.

Adjectives in Irish go **after** the noun ('a car black').

black
dubh
*a **black** car*
*carr **dubh***

The spelling of an adjective can change when a noun is feminine or plural.

'A big window' is **fuinneog mhór**, 'the blue sky' is **an spéir ghorm**, and 'a clean shirt' is **léine ghlan**, because the nouns being described are feminine.

white
bán
*I'm wearing a **white** shirt.*
*Léine **bhán** atá orm.*

'A town' is **baile mór** (**m**) , and 'towns' is **bailte móra**. 'The blue shirt' is **an léine ghorm** (**f**) , and 'the blue shirts' is **na léinte gorma**. It does not matter if these nouns are masculine or feminine. As long as they are plural, the adjectives describing them are plural.

Verbs

Words such as 'eat' or 'see' are **verbs** or doing words.

Verbs in Irish come at the beginning of a sentence. 'The cat **is** under the table' is **Tá** an cat faoin tábla.

The ends of verbs change depending on who or what is doing the action. Here are a few of the main Irish verbs

bí	**to be**	**déan**	**to do**
tá mé	I am	déan**aim**	I do
tá tú	you are	déan**ann** tú	you do
tá sé	he is	déan**ann** sé	he does
tá sí	she is	déan**ann** sí	she does
táimid	we are	déan**aimid**	we do
tá sibh	you are	déan**ann** sibh	you do
tá siad	they are	déan**ann** siad	they do
bheith istigh	**to be** inside	cleachtaí **a dhéanamh**	**to do** exercises

can	**to sing**	**scríobh**	**to write**
can**aim**	I sing	scríobh**aim**	I write
can**ann** tú	you sing	scríobh**ann** tú	you write
can**ann** sé	he sings	scríobh**ann** sé	he writes
can**ann** sí	she sings	scríobh**ann** sí	she writes
can**aimid**	we sing	scríobh**aimid**	we write
can**ann** sibh	you sing	scríobh**ann** sibh	you write
can**ann** siad	they sing	scríobh**ann** siad	they write
Is maith liom **canadh.**	I like **to sing.**	Tá mé **ag scríobh.**	I am **writing.**

téigh	**to go**	**foghlaim**	**to learn**
téim	I go	foghlaim**ím**	I learn
téann tú	you go	foghlaim**íonn** tú	you learn
téann sé	he goes	foghlaim**íonn** sé	he learns
téann sí	she goes	foghlaim**íonn** sí	she learns
téimid	we go	foghlaim**ímid**	we learn
téann sibh	you go	foghlaim**íonn** sibh	you learn
téann siad	they go	foghlaim**íonn** siad	they learn
Tá mam **ag dul** amach.	Mum's **going** out.	Tá sí **ag foghlaim** dabhsa.	She's **learning** to dance.

All verbs in this dictionary have an example to show you how to use them.

Index

A, a

abair: **say**

abhainn *f* (aibhneacha): **river**

aerfort *m*: **airport**

aghaidh *f* (aghaidheanna): **face**

agus: **and**

aibítir *f*: **alphabet**

ainm *m* (ainmneacha): **name**

ainmhí *m* (ainmhithe): **animal**

airgead *m*: **money**

airgead póca *m*: **pocket money**

amárach: **tomorrow**

amharc: **look**

an-: **very**

anois: **now**

anraith *m*: **soup**

anseo: **here**

aon: **one, only**

arán *m*: **bread**

ard: **loud, tall**

arís: **again**

athair *m* (aithreacha): **father**

B, b

bábóg *f*: **doll**

bád *m*: **boat**

baile mór *m* (bailte móra): **town**

bainne *m*: **milk**

balla *m*: **wall**

balún *m*: **balloon**

bán: **white**

banaltra *f*: **nurse**

banana *m*: **banana**

banphrionsa *m*: **princess**

banríon *f* (banríonacha): **queen**

beag: **little**

béal *m*: **mouth**

bean *f* (mná): **lady, woman**

bean chéile *f* (mná céilí): **wife**

béic: **shout**

béile *m*: **meal**

béirín *m*: **teddy bear**

bia *m*: **food**

bialann *f*: **restaurant**

blaincéad *m*: **blanket**

bláth *m* (bláthanna): **flower**

bliain *f* (blianta): **year**

bó *f* (ba): **cow**

bosca *m*: **box**

bóthar *m* (bóithre): **road**

bréagán *m*: **toy**

breithlá *m*: **birthday**

bricfeasta *m*: **breakfast**

brionglóid *f*: **dream**

brístí gearra *pl*: **shorts**

brístí géine *pl*: **jeans**

bróg *f*: **shoe**

bronntanas *m*: **present**

buaigh: **win**

buail le: **meet**

buaiteoir *m*: **winner**

buartha: **sad**

buatais *f*: **boot**

bugaí linbh *m*: **pushchair**

buí: **yellow**

buicéad *m*: **bucket**

burgar *m*: **burger**

bus *m* (busanna): **bus**

C, c

cáca *m*: **cake**

caife *m*: **coffee**

cailín *m*: **girl**

caill: **lose**

cailleach *f*: **witch**

caillte: **lost**

caipín *m*: **cap**

cairéad *m*: **carrot**

cairpéad *m*: **carpet**

cáis *f*: **cheese**

caisleán *m*: **castle**

caith: **wear**

callán *m*: **noise**

can: **sing**

caora *f* (caoirigh): **sheep**

caora fíniúna *pl*: **grapes**

capaillín *m*: **pony**

capall *m*: **horse**

cara *m* (cairde): **friend**

carbhat *m*: **tie**

carr *m* (carranna): **car**

cárta *m*: **card**

cárta poist *m*: **postcard**

cat *m*: **cat**

cathaoir *f* (cathaoireacha): **chair**

cathaoir rothaí *f* (cathaoireacha rothaí): **wheelchair**

céad: **first; hundred**

ceamara gréasáin *m*: **webcam**

ceann *m* (cinn): **head**

céanna: **same**

ceannach: **buy, buying**

ceapaire *m*: **sandwich**

cearnóg *f*: **square**

ceart: **right**

ceol *m*: **music**

cineálta: **kind**

ciorcal *m*: **circle**

cipíní itheacháin *pl*: **chopsticks**

ciseán *m*: **basket**

cistin *f* (cistineacha): **kitchen**

cithfholcadán *m*: **shower**

cleachtadh *m* (cleachtaí): **exercise**

cloch *f*: **stone**

clog *m*: **clock**

cluas: **ear**

cluiche *m*: **game**

cluin: **hear**

codail: **sleep**

cógais *pl*: **medicine**

coileán *m*: **puppy**

coinín *m*: **rabbit**

coinneal *f* (coinnle): **candle**

coinnigh: **keep**

cóisir *f*: **party**

comharsa *f* (comharsana): **neighbour**

contúirteach: **dangerous**

corp *m*: **body**

cos *f*: **leg, foot**

cóta *m*: **coat**

craiceann *m* (craicne): **skin**

crann *m*: **tree**

crua: **hard**

cuileog *f*: **fly**

cuir: **send**

cuirtín *m*: **curtain**

cuisneoir *m*: **fridge**

D, d

daid *m* (daideanna): **dad**

damhán alla *m*: **spider**

daoine *pl*: **people**

dara: **second**

de: **of**

deacair: **difficult**

déan: **do, make**

déan deifir: **hurry up**

déan gáire: **laugh**

dearg: **red**

deartháir *m* (deartháireacha): **brother**

deas: **nice**

deilf *f* (deilfeanna): **dolphin**

deireadh seachtaine *m* (deirí seachtaine): **weekend**

deirfiúr *f* (deirfiúracha): **sister**

dia duit: **hello**

dineasár *m*: **dinosaur**

dinnéar: **dinner**

díol: **sell**

dochtúir *m*: **doctor**

an Domhan: **Earth**

domhan *m*: **world**

doras *m* (doirse): **door**

dragan *m*: **dragon**

draíodóir *m*: **magician**

droch-: **bad**

droichead *m*: **bridge**

dubh: **black**

duine fásta *m* (daoine fásta): **adult**

DVD *m* (DVD-anna): **DVD**

E, e

eachtrán *m*: **alien**

éadaí *pl*: **clothes**

éan *m*: **bird**

éide *f*: **uniform**

eile: **other**

eilifint *f*: **elephant**

éist: **listen**

eitleán *m*: **plane**

eitleog *f*: **kite**

eochair *f* (eochracha): **key**

F, f

faigh: **find**

fáilte: **welcome**

fáinne *m*: **ring**

fan: **wait**

fanaile *m*: **vanilla**

farraige *f*: **sea**

fás: **grow**

fathach *m*: **giant**

fear *m* (fir): **man**

féar *m*: **grass**

fear céile *m* (fir chéili): **husband**

fear grinn *m* (fir ghrinn): **clown**

fear poist *m* (fir phoist): **postman**

fear sneachta *m* (fir shneachta): **snowman**

fearthainn *f*: **rain**

feic: **see**

féileacán *m*: **butterfly**

féilire *m*: **calendar**

feisteas *m*: **costume**

feithid *f*: **insect**

feoil *f*: **meat**

fiacail *f* (fiacla): **tooth**

fiafraigh de: **ask**

fiáin: **wild**

físchluiche *m*: **video game**

focal *m*: **word**

foclóir *m*: **dictionary**

foghlaí mara *m*: **pirate**

foghlaim: **learn**

folamh: **empty**

folcadán *m*: **bath**

foraois *f*: **forest**

forc *m*: **fork**

frog *m* (froganna): **frog**

fuar: **cold**

fuinneog *f*: **window**

furasta: **easy**

G, g

gabhar *m*: **goat**

gach: **every**

gaineamh *m*: **sand**

gairdín *m*: **garden**

gallúnach *f*: **soap**

gan: **without**

gaoth *f*: **wind**

garáiste *m*: **garage**

gasta: **quick**

gasúr *m*: **boy**

gealach *f*: **moon**

giotár *m*: **guitar**

glan: **clean**

glaoigh ar: **call**

glasra *m*: **vegetable**

gleoite: **pretty**

gliú *m*: **glue**

gloine *f*: **glass**

gluaisrothar *m*: **motorbike**

glúin *f* (glúine): **knee**

go gasta: **fast**

go maith: **well**

go raibh maith agat: **thank you**

goil: **cry**

gorm: **blue**

gráinneog *f*: **hedgehog**

greamaigh: **stick**

greamán *m*: **sticker**

greannmhar: **funny**

grian *f*: **sun**

grianghraf *m*: **photo**

gruagaire *m*: **hairdresser**

gruaig *f*: **hair**

gúna *m*: **dress**

guthán *m*: **telephone**

H, h

hamstar *m*: **hamster**

hata *m*: **hat**

héileacaptar *m*: **helicopter**

I, i

i ndiaidh: **after**

iasc *m* (éisc): **fish**

iasc órga *m* (éisc órga): **goldfish**

im *m*: **butter**

imir: **play**

iníon *f* (iníonacha): **daughter**

inné: **yesterday**

inniu: **today**

ith: **eat**

J, j

jab *m* (jabanna): **job**

L, l

lá *m* (laethanta): **day**

lacha *f* (lachain): **duck**

láidir: **strong**

lámh *f* (lámha): **arm, hand**

lampa *m*: **lamp**

lán: **full**

le: **with**

le chéile: **together**

leaba *f* (leapacha): **bed**

leabhar *m*: **book**

leanbh *m* (leanaí): **baby**

leathanach *m*: **page**

léigh: **read**

léim: **jump**

léine *f* (léinte): **shirt**

leithreas *m*: **toilet**

leon *m*: **lion**

linn snámha *f* (linnte snámha): **swimming pool**

líomóid *f*: **lemon**

litir *f* (litreacha): **letter**

loch *m* (lochanna): **lake**

lón *m* (lónta): **lunch**

luchóg *f*: **mouse**

M, m

mac *m* (mic): **son**

mac tíre *m* (mic thíre): **wolf**

madra *m*: **dog**

maidin *f* (maidineacha): **morning**

maighdean mhara *f*: **mermaid**

maith: **good**

mála *m*: **bag**

mall: **late, slow**

mam *f* (mamanna): **mum**

margadh *m* (margaí): **market**

máthair *f* (máithreacha): **mother**

méar *f*: **finger**

mí *f* (míonna): **month**

mícheart: **wrong**

milseog *f*: **dessert**

miongháire *m*: **smile**

miotóg *f*: **glove**

míreanna mearaí *pl*: **jigsaw**

moncaí *m*: **monkey**

mór: **big**

mórán: **many**

muc ghuine *f*: **guinea pig**

múscail: **wake up**

N, n

nathair *f* (nathracha): **snake**

nigh: **wash**

níos lú: **less**

níos mó: **more**

nuachtán *m*: **newspaper**

O, o

ó: **from**

obair: **work**

obair bhaile *f*: **homework**

óg: **young**

oíche *f* (oícheanta): **night**

oileán *m*: **island**

ól: **drink**

ollmhargadh *m* (ollmhargaí): **supermarket**

ollphéist *f* (ollphéisteanna): **monster**

oscail: **open**

ospidéal *m*: **hospital**

otharcharr *m* (otharcharranna): **ambulance**

P, p

páipéar *m*: **paper**

páirc *f* (páirceanna): **park**

páirc súgartha *f* (páirceanna súgartha): **playground**

páiste *m*: **child, kid**

pas *m* (pasanna): **passport**

pasta *m*: **pasta**

peann *m* (pinn): **pen**

peann luaidhe *m* (pinn luaidhe): **pencil**

peata *m*: **pet**

peil *f*: **ball, football**

péinteáil: **paint**

pianó *m* (pianónna): **piano**

picnic *f*: **picnic**

pictiúr *m*: **picture**

pictiúrlann *f*: **cinema**

piscín *m*: **kitten**

piseanna *pl*: **peas**

pitseámaí *pl*: **pyjamas**

pizza *m*: **pizza**

planda *m*: **plant**

pláta *m*: **plate**

póca *m*: **pocket**

póg *f*: **kiss**

póilín *m*: **policeman**

praiseach *f*: **mess**

práta *m*: **potato**

prionsa *m*: **prince**

puipéad *m*: **puppet**

R, r

raidió *m*: **radio**

rás *m*: **race**

réalta *f*: **star**

réidh: **ready**

rí *m* (ríthe): **king**

ríomhaire *m*: **computer**

ríomhaire glúine *m*: **laptop**

ríomhphost *m*: **email**

rís *f*: **rice**

rith: **run**

robat *m*: **robot**

roicéad *m*: **rocket**

roimh: **before**

rothar *m*: **bicycle**

rud ar bith: **nothing**

S, s

saibhir: **rich**

salach: **dirty**

saoire *f*: **holiday**

scamall *m*: **cloud**

scáth m (scáthanna): shadow

scáth fearthainne m (scáthanna fearthainne): umbrella

scéal m (scéalta): story

scian f (sceana): knife

sciorta m: skirt

scoil f (scoileanna): school

scríobh: write

scuab fiacla f: toothbrush

séabra m: zebra

seachtain f (seachtainí): week

seacláid f: chocolate

seaicéad m: jacket

sean: old

seilide m: snail

seomra m: room

seomra leapa m: bedroom

seomra ranga m: classroom

sicín m: chicken

sióg f: fairy

siopa m: shop

sioráf m: giraffe

siosúr sg: scissors

siúil: walk

slán: goodbye

sliabh m (sléibhte): mountain

smaoineamh m (smaointe): idea

smaoinigh: think

sneachta m: snow

solas m (soilse): light

sona: happy

sorcas m: circus

spasárthach m: spaceship

spéaclaí pl: glasses

spéir f (spéartha): sky

spórt m: sport

spúnóg f: spoon

sráid f (sráideanna): street

srón f: nose

stad: stop

staighre m: stairs

stáisiún m: station

stoca m: sock

stór m (stórtha): treasure

sú m: juice

suaimhneach: quiet

suas staighre: upstairs

subh f: jam

suigh: sit

súil f (súile): eye

suíomh gréasáin m (suíomha gréasáin): website

T, t

T-léine f (T-léinte): T-shirt

tabhair: bring, give

tábla m: table

tacsaí m: taxi

tae m: tea

taibhse f: ghost

taispeáin: show

talamh m (tailte): ground

taos fiacla m: toothpaste

tar: come

tarracóir m: tractor

tarraing: draw

te: hot, warm

teach m (tithe): house

teachtaireacht téacs f: text message

teaghlach m: family

téigh: go

teilifís f: television

thíos staighre: downstairs

tine f (tinte): fire

tinn: sick

tinte ealaíne pl: fireworks

tíogar m: tiger

tóg: take

toirtís f: tortoise

tolg m: sofa

tonn f (tonnta): wave

toradh m (torthaí): fruit

tósta m: toast

trá f (tránna): beach

traein f (traenacha): train

tráta m: tomato

tráthnóna m (tráthnónta): afternoon, evening

treabhsar m: trousers

tréidlia m (tréidlianna): vet

triantán m: triangle

tríú: third

tuáille m: towel

tuar ceatha m (tuartha ceatha): rainbow

an tuath: countryside

tuig: understand

tuismitheoirí pl: parents

U, u

uachtar reoite m: ice cream

uair an chloig f (uaireanta an chloig): hour

uaireadóir m: watch

uan m: lamb

ubh f (uibheacha): egg

uimhir f (uimhreacha): number

uisce m: water

úll m (úlla): apple

urlár m: floor

V, v

vardrús m: wardrobe

X, x

x-gha m (x-gathanna): X-ray

xileafón m: xylophone

Z, z

zú m (zúnna): zoo